Cougar

Children Book of Fun Facts & Amazing Photos on Animals in Nature - A Wonderful Cougar Book for Kids aged 3-7

By

Ina Felix

Ina Felix

Copyright © 2015 by Ina Felix

All rights reserved. No part of this book may be used or reproduced in any manner whatsoever without the express written permission of the publisher except for the use of brief quotations in a book review. Image Credits: Royalty free images reproduced under license from various stock image repositories. Under a creative commons licenses.

I am a cougar.

I am also known as a mountain lion or puma.

I am a mammal like dogs, cows, and bears.

I can be found all around the Americas.

I can live in mountains, plains, and even deserts.

I am closely related to cats just like jaguars, leopards, and lions.

I am the second heaviest cat in the Americas next to the jaguar.

I look like a lion but our males do not have manes.

I love to hunt prey just like other carnivores.

I cleverly hunt without being seen by my prey.

I use my sharp claws when I attack my prey.

I love to eat meat.

My favorite preys are sheep, rodents, and moose.

Sometimes I share the land with other fellow predators like grizzly bears and wolves.

My fur is sometimes brownish-orange, reddish, or silver gray.

I can grow very tall — up to 9 feet.

I cannot roar but I can purr like small cats.

I can climb mountains well using my paws.

Cougar females can give birth up to three kittens.

I can live up to 20 years old.

I hope you had fun learning about my family.

Thank you.

Made in the USA
San Bernardino, CA
02 August 2016